# UNDERCOVER

Understanding and
Receiving the Benefits
of Spiritual Covering

**PAUL WONDRACEK**

*PAUL WONDRACEK*

# UNDERCOVER

Understanding and Receiving
the Benefits of Spiritual
Covering...

By: Paul Wondracek

**Copyright © 2021 by Paul Wondracek**
All publishing rights belong exclusively to Wondracek Ministries International
All rights reserved. No part of this publication may be reproduced or transmitted in any form or by any means, electronic or mechanical, including photocopy, recording, or any information storage and retrieval system, without permission in writing from the copyright owner.

*Printed in the United States of America*

# TABLE OF CONTENTS
≈≈≈≈

| | |
|---|---|
| Only Covered Seeds Grow | 9 |
| The Role of Leadership in Your Life | 23 |
| The Orphan Spirit | 37 |
| Fathers Help You Finish | 53 |
| The Pursuit | 69 |
| The Divine Equation of Wealth | 83 |
| 100 Power Quotes about Covering | 101 |

*PAUL WONDRACEK*

# ACKNOWLEDGMENTS

I would like to thank My Lord Jesus Christ for taking this shy little boy and turning him into a strong confident man. Through many betrayals and hardships I am who I am in Him. Thank you to my wife for your love, understanding, and support of my calling and purpose. Thank you to the mentors in my life who have spent hours sharing The Word of God together over phone calls and meals.

## ∞ 1 ∞

# Only Covered Seeds Grow

~~~~~

One of my favorite passages in the Bible is about the four soils. Jesus taught us about the four souls and how each affects the seed of the Word of God in our lives. We live in a time where a lot of negative things are being said about spiritual covering and an independent spirit has infiltrated the Church where everyone believes that all they need is a good sermon on Sunday morning and they will become all that God wants them to be.

This couldn't be further from the truth. God moves through delegated authority that he put in place. When you violate the chain of command in the Bible there is always a price to pay for it. Only covered seeds grow! Matthew 13:3 tells us, *"Then he told them many things in parables, saying, "3 A farmer went out to sow his seed. 4 As he was scattering the seed, some fell among the path, and the birds came and ate it up. 5 Some fell on rocky places, where it did not have much soil. It sprang up quickly, because the soil was shallow. 6 But when the sun came up the plants were scorched, and they withered because they had no root. 7 Other seed fell among the thorns, which grew up and choked the plants. 8 Still other seed fell on good soil, where it produced a crop, a hundred, sixty, or thirty times what was sown."*

  This famous passage is amazing because it shows us the importance of spiritual covering. Of all the four different types of soil three of the four could not be covered. Only in one of the soils was the seed able to produce and it was the soil that the seed could be covered with. You cannot cover a seed on the path, nor in the rocks, nor among the thorns. The difference in the soil was how the seed was able to develop roots and only the good soil was able to allow the seed to develop roots.

  Because the good soil protected the seed. When a seed is uncovered it is left to the elements as this passage indicated. It is left to the birds to steal, the sun to scorch, and the thorns to choke. But when a seed is covered it is protected. Spiritual covering in your life is all about protection. The prodigal son wanted to leave the Father's house and go out on his own.

He wanted the blessing of the Father without the presence of the Father. He wanted covenant without covering. He learned the hard way about going at life alone and isolated. It didn't work out too well for him.

Covering brings legitimacy. An uncovered seed is illegitimate. Here are the seven benefits of soil as a covering...

> ➤ Protects (from elements storm flood)
> ➤ Extracts (the potential of the seed)
> ➤ Feeds (nourishes the seed)
> ➤ Connects (develops a root system)
> ➤ Comforts (keeps the seed warm)
> ➤ Waters (holds the water in)
> ➤ Propels (pushes the seed upward)

As the soil does this to the seed so the spiritual covering does this to your life. Once you plant yourself into the proper soil or covering what God put in you will begin to flourish.

First the soil protects the seed. The right spiritual covering brings protection to your house. Covering is all about protection! If we look at the famous flood in the Bible found in Genesis the whole earth was flooded with water and all of humanity was destroyed except 8 people which were Noah and his family.

What is interesting to note is that Noah new the flood was over when he sent out the dove to find vegetation. Genesis 8:8 tells us, *"Then he sent out a dove to see if the water had receded from the surface of the ground. 9 But the Dove could find nowhere to perch because there was water all over the surface of the earth, so it returned to Noah in the ark. He reached out his hand and took the Dove and brought it back to himself in the ark. 10 He waited seven more days and again sent out the Dove from the ark. 11 When the Dove returned to him in the evening, there in its beak was a freshly plucked olive leaf! Then Noah knew that the water had receded from the earth. 12 He waited seven more days and sent the Dove out again, but this time it did not return to him."*

So we see here that the Dove eventually brought back an olive leaf. Wait a minute I thought that the whole earth was destroyed by water and everyone in it? It was but that olive leaf was proof of one thing. It was proof that a covered seed is always protected. Everything above the ground was destroyed by the flood but the storm couldn't touch what was under the ground.

The seed! The seed was covered by the ground so that even the flood was not able to penetrate the ground and destroy the seed. When you are covered by God's divine delegated authority even the storm cannot destroy the seed inside of you. Noah started looking around and seeing all the vegetation and trees growing once again.

He even planted a vineyard and began to see the seeds produce once again. No matter what you go through in life when you are properly covered by godly mentorship the seeds inside of you will grow again. The end is not really the end. When you think it is over realize it is getting ready to begin again, why? Because the covered seed will always grow again.

The seeds that have been planted inside of you are protected by the covering of the soil of mentorship and leadership and they are safe. The seed of God in you does not keep you from making mistakes but it does cause you to make things right when you do mess up and not turn it into a lifestyle. Everyone lies at some point in their life, but some people are liars. Meaning that is the language that they speak.

Lying is not a mistake that they made but it has now become a lifestyle that they live. There is a big difference. When someone who has the seed of God in them sins they are quick to make it right and see the error of their ways.

They cannot live low. Life calls them higher because they live under command. The command of God lives inside of them in their DNA. DNA is nothing more than written instructions from your lineage. DNA is the commands written in your genes to produce brown hair or blue eyes,

God's seed through Christ is in your very DNA commanding you to live Holy, walk in favor. Living low is not in your DNA if the seed of God is in you and the blessing of God is on you.

God didn't have to plant grass twice. He said "Let there be..." one time and there was. He didn't have to wake up every morning and say "Let there be grass" again. He put a seed in it. God doesn't have to save you over and over He put His seed in you it keeps germinating. God doesn't have to bless you again every day. He blessed you once in Christ and that seed now lives in you continuously perpetuating the blessing of God in your life every day that you wake up.

That is why the famous scripture says in Lamentations 3:23, *"His mercies are new every morning."* The seed of mercy has been planted inside of you through Christ and every morning that you wake up new mercy has sprung up while you were sleeping.

The seed of God is growing while you are sleeping. The seed of the Kingdom of God is working in you while you are not even aware of what is happening. As you continue to feed your faith with the Word and water it with the presence of God, new mercy and grace will spring up every day.

Seeds may lie dormant but they don't die. They just spring up the next season that comes around. The grass might turn brown and look like it is dead but it's not dead its just dormant and when the sun starts shining and the rains start falling the seed wakes up again and starts to grow.

I came here to tell someone that the seed of God inside of you is not dead it is just lying dormant because of what you went through and because of some of the decisions that you made, but every dormant seed comes alive in a new season. The things that you thought were dead are coming to life again and waking up. New mercy and new favor are overtaking your life because the dormant seeds have been awakened by the Word of God. Some seeds spring up suddenly.

Take the bamboo plant for instance. Once the Bamboo seed is planted it sits in the soil for 3 years and nothing happens. No growth and no sign of life. Once the bamboo seed is planted it is working under the ground where no one can see. When the seed of God is in your life it may seem like nothing is happening, but something is happening where no one can see.

Once the third year ends the Bamboo seed springs up suddenly and grows 90 feet in three months. God doesn't do things fast but He does do them suddenly. The seeds that you thought were doing nothing inside of you are suddenly about to spring forth with life, favor, and creativity.

God is about to do a suddenly in your life. That means that He was working all along but now He is just going to let everyone else see what He has been doing the whole time. That is what a suddenly is all about.

Everything is in you in seed form awaiting your entry into the proper environment or climate. You may have the seeds of greatness inside of you but if you never enter the environment or climate of the Kingdom those seeds may never grow. You may have the bad seed of alcoholism inside of you but it will not activate until you enter an environment that feed that seed. If you want a seed to die just put it in the wrong environment. Climate determines cultivation and environment decides what grows.

Here are seven seeds that God planted in your life and the environment that you place yourself in determines whether or not these seeds with spring up.

- The Seed of Faith
- The Seed of the Kingdom
- The Seed of Potential
- The Seed of Righteousness
- The Seed of Greatness
- The Seed of Victory
- The Seed of Favor

Every seed needs the proper environment to grow. The good seeds grow in the good climate and the bad seeds grow in the wrong climates. The environment that you create determines the product you produce. If you don't like what's growing inside of you then check your surroundings. Check the environment that you have decided to remain in.

Even in the natural there are different types of seed and these seeds grow in different kinds of environments. Take grass for instance. There are seven types of grass seeds and each on grows in a different environment and takes a different type of cultivation. Here are the 7 types of grass seeds and how each one grows in a different environment...

➤ Tall Fescue (Durable grows in shade)
➤ Bermuda (Thrives in challenging climates)
➤ Centipede (Weed resistant)
➤ Zoysia (Tolerates cold longevity)
➤ Rye grass (Resists insects)
➤ Kentucky Blue Grass (Rebounds strong)
➤ Bahia grass (disease resistant)

Each one of these seeds grows in a different environment and has different characteristics just like the seeds that God has planted inside of you. Let's look at each one.
Tall fescue is a durable grass and it grows in shade. There are some seeds in your life that will even grow in a dark place. In fact some seeds grow better in a dark place. When you are going through a trial or a season of struggle your seeds will begin to spring forth during a season of struggle.
Faith grows best in times of struggle. Faith that is not tested cannot be trusted. When you are in a dark place your faith will soar because all you have to hang on to is the promise of God. It is important in a season like this to surround yourself with people of faith. Light shines best in darkness. The next see is called Bermuda. Just like fescue Bermuda grass

thrives in challenging climates. This seed will even begin to grow in your life when you are surrounded by worldly doubting people. People who don't know your God and don't believe His promises. Your faith will soar anyways.

If you have to be around an environment where people don't believe your God there are some seed in you that will grow despite the negative climate. That is the power of the seed of God.

The next type of grass is Centipede. Centipede is weed resistant. There are some seeds in your life that will not give into sin, doubt, or unbelief. The weeds of worldly temptation will not affect you as you press on in God. Some seeds resist weeds.

The next grass seed is Zoysia. Zoysia tolerated cold and has longevity. Some seeds in your life will hang on for a long time. Seeds that you thought were long dead but only lying dormant and God is waking them up to being you a harvest of Kingdom blessing.

They resist cold and negative attitudes. When the seed of God is in you. You have joy when others give in to negativity.

The next seed is Rye Grass. Rye Grass is resistant to insects. There are some seeds that demons cannot touch. No matter what the devil puts you through the seed of God remains in you. The Word of God in you resists the enemy's advances. The Bible says in James 4:7, *"Resist the devil and he will flee from you."* In other words when your life is submitted to God and

you resist the enemy he cannot touch the seed on your life. The dream seeds, the faith seeds, the vision seeds that God has planted inside of you.
 The next grass seed is Kentucky Bluegrass. This grass seed is known to rebound strong. When life knocks you down you always bounce back stronger than before. You have a bounce back Anointing. It is not how hard you hit the devil that makes you strong it's how hard your enemy can hit you and you still keep bouncing back.
 The final seed is the Bahai Grass. Bahai Grass is disease resistant. When the seed of God is in you there are some things that cannot stick to you. Plagues that cannot come near your house because Psalm 91 tells is that God will keep you from the pestilence and plague.
 Things that would've killed others cannot even come near you because the seed of God is in you. When you live under the right covering you realize that the seed of God is in your life and the blessing of God is on your life.
 This is the importance of having the proper covering in your life. God does everything through delegated chain of command and the seeds in your life will begin to spring forth when you connect with the proper covering and mentorship in your life.

*Pray with me*

*Father thank you for the seeds of potential that you have placed inside of me. Connect me with the proper covering and mentorship in my life so that I can thrive and flourish like you have promised me in your Word in Jesus Name Amen!*

# Chapter Review and Key Points

- When a seed is uncovered it is left to the elements as this passage indicated. It is left to the birds to steal, the sun to scorch, and the thorns to choke. But when a seed is covered it is protected. Spiritual covering in your life is all about protection.

- The seed was covered by the ground so that event the flood was not able to penetrate the ground and destroy the seed. When you are covered by God's divine delegated authority even the storm cannot destroy the seed inside of you. Noah started looking around and seeing all the vegetation and trees growing once again.

- Every seed needs the proper environment to grow. The good seeds grow in the good climate and the bad seeds grow in the wrong climates. The environment that you create determines the product you produce. If you don't like what's growing inside of you then check your surroundings.

Check the environment that you have decided to remain in.

## 2

# The Role of Leadership in Your Life

This has been a confusing and often painful topic in people's lives. The role of leadership and its purpose in our lives. Leadership is one thing and one thing only. Creating positive change in someone's life. John Quincy Adams famously said, "If your actions inspire others to dream more, learn more, do more, ad become more, you are a leader." Somebody who has something that you don't have knows something that you don't know.

Many people have a skewed view of leadership because of their relationship with their father or a bad experience with leadership in their lives. A leader has been where you are going and has made the mistakes that you are about to make. A better word for leadership in my mind is mentorship. Many are confused about the purpose of leadership in your life. In the last chapter we discussed what the covering or leader does for the seed now I want to take a minute and discuss what the leader does not do...

- Leaders don't meddle they pray
- Leaders don't dictate they inspire
- Leaders don't control they suggest
- Leaders don't ignore they engage
- Leaders don't take advantage they give it
- Leaders don't demand honor they identify it
- Leaders don't give answers they inspire pursuit

We often talk about the good qualities of leadership but fail to discuss the unsavory experiences that we have had with bad leadership. So the list above was inspired by my bad experiences with leadership that helped to shape me as a leader.
First Leaders don't meddle they pray. We've all suffered at the hands of insecure leadership. Leaders that need the ego boost and have to be made to feel important all the time. Leaders who do what I call meddling. What is meddling? Meddling is when a leader has to know every detail of his people's lives.
He wants to know what they think and what they are saying all the time. He wants all the details of their crisis and tells them what

they need to do in black and white. He gets involved in their emotional storm and sees their problems as his problems. This type of leader always wants to know what is going on and may even have people spy on and surveil his people for information. We as leaders are not called to meddle in people's lives. We are not called to give advice where it has not been sought.

Yes we have to check on people and feel out where they may be at but that is done subtly and with respect. It is called being political not in the bad sense but in the leadership sense. There are two kinds of people in this world those who initiate and those who react. We must learn to check on the people we care about and lead without seeming to violate their privacy.

That is the difference between the person who stays in their office and talks to no one and really doesn't even say hello when walking to their office, and the person who sticks their head in the door of their supervisor's office and says, "Everything ok today?', "Anything you need help with"?

Here are 7 ways to care for someone without meddling...

➢ Let them know you're checking on them
➢ Ask how their spouse or family are
➢ Ask if there is anything you can pray about
➢ Never act shocked when someone reveals a bad decision
➢ Keep it light
➢ Don't offer advice unless asked for

> Let them know they were on your heart today

These may seem like small things but they let people know that you care in a special way for them as a leader. People forget what you say and what you do, but they will never forget how you made them feel.

Here are seven examples of meddling behavior from leaders...

> Arguing with your people
> Asking about personal things
> Throwing scripture at them
> Making personal loans to them
> Telling them what to do
> Forbidding them to do certain things
> Constantly correcting them

This has been a popular topic in leadership today especially in the Church world. There is an over emphasis on correction. I've been to the meetings and watched what goes on there and most of it is an ego trip.

Great leaders don't spend their time always correcting their people but encouraging them. That may sound something like, "That is not something I would do", rather than, "that is a terrible decision". See the difference. Great leaders can correct you and make it feel like you have just been encouraged.

Which brings me to the 2nd characteristic of true leadership. Leaders don't dictate they INSPIRE! Leaders who go around shouting orders are not leaders they are people who carry a title and take themselves way too seriously. Good leaders inspire others. Dictator leaders don't last long. Dictator leaders might be followed and obeyed but they will often not be lived or trusted very much.

If I make someone do something I have to continue to tell them what to do. If I inspire someone to do something they become self motivated and don't need reminding but develop the passion because they understand more than just the "What", they understand the "Why" behind the instruction and the inspiration.

It is not anyone job to inspire you, and it is not God's job to inspire you. It is your job to FIND what inspires you and put it in front of you. As leaders our job is to help people find what inspires them and help them get there.

Now I love number three. Leaders don't control they suggest. We are not out here trying to make clones of ourselves. The greatest thing a leader can do is make a suggestion. Suggestions are received easier than commands. We are not God. He is the only one that should give commands.

I'm amazed when I see pastors give their leaders commands and want to be involved in all their members life decisions. This is a very dangerous thing to do. When someone comes to you and asks you, "What should I do?" You should never tell them what they should do. As discussed earlier a leader should always say something like, *"That is not something I would do"*. Or even, *"If I were in your position I would probably do this"*. Giving people commands is always going to be counterproductive and backfire on a leader because when they do what you commanded and don't get the results that you promised they are going to blame you for giving them bad advice.

Number four leaders don't ignore they engage. It is very popular today for leaders to hide in the back office and never touch or engage with their people. It is important to initiate with your people. Avoid leaders who hide and never engage with their people. Jesus was not like this.

Jesus was in the marketplace engaging with the people healing them and loving on them. Access is important and leaders must learn proper boundaries but it is very important to reach out and speak to your people. Walk slowly through the crowd and greet people not always of course but from time to time.

Introverted leaders often find engaging with their people difficult. Introverted people often find disengagement easy. Introverted people tend to live in a state of disengagement instead of finding where they are naturally extroverted they never really discover where they engage the best.

Some have extroverted personalities and no one is a stranger. They share love and affection very easily. Extroverted personalities know how to make people feel important and valuable. They are great natural leaders. But one can also be extroverted in their creativity. You may not be the life of the party but you have a special gift to be creative and your extroversion comes out in your creative expression. You're still an extrovert just in a different area of your life. Some are spiritually extroverted. They love to talk about spiritual things and like myself write books and dive deep into the study of the Bible.

Others can be extroverted in productivity. They get the job done. They are finishers! These people love to stay busy. They might not say much but they let their work do the talking. Others can be extroverted in their priorities. They are goal setters and are quick to teach others the best way to do things. These people understand structure and strategy and make good managers.

They are organizationally expressive and find a place for everything. Still other can be extroverted in their comradery. They are relational and make friends easily. These people are socially extroverted and consider spending time with others a great investment. Finally there are those that are expressive in their polarity. They are not afraid to disagree. They always offer a perspective that may be different from others and challenges the status quo.

Just because one is not extroverted in their personality does not mean that they are not extroverted in one of these areas. Sometimes being introverted is nothing more than a comfort zone and an excuse for being disengaged. Find where you are extroverted and be expressive to those around you. Someone needs what you have. Someone cannot start unless you finish.

Many leaders have disengaged and become introverted because of the disloyalty of others. Leaders who often hide in their offices are facing some rejection issues that make it difficult for them to engage with their people.

I'm going to skip to number six because it flows well with the last one we discussed. Leaders don't demand honor they identify it. One of the problems that we have seen in modern day leadership especially in the Church is the demanding of honor.

Honor that is demanded is fake honor. Honor that comes from the heart is genuine. You cannot make people respect you and you cannot make someone love you. These are an act of the human will. Leaders who demand honor are going down a wrong path.

Honor must be identified not demanded. In other words who do you see that has genuine honor and respect for you and your gift? Once you identify honor in another you can begin to trust them more and more with leadership responsibility. Pour into those who show honor. Invest in those who show a hunger to learn and an interest in serving your vision.

Don't demand honor from people who have not discovered your difference. Don't sit under leadership who demand honor and respect. That

is a dictator and if this is the way that you behave as a leader then you're in for a tough journey. Remember dictatorships don't last. They get toppled. No dictatorship in history has remained for a long time. It is self-destructive leadership. Hitler, Mussolini, and other dictatorships in the world have not stayed in power long.
Punishing people because they don't show you honor is toxic and destructive. If you see dishonor just move away from it. If you identify honor pull it closer and invest into it. But do not force people to act in a way that is contrary to how they really feel in their hearts. Here are seven honoring characteristics to identify...

➢ The willingness to learn from you
➢ Expression of gratitude
➢ Inquiring about how to help
➢ Brand evangelists
➢ Financial support
➢ Showing up and engaging with others
➢ Reaching out to you to solve problems

These are powerful ways to show honor to a leader and these are things that leaders should identify as signs of honor and move towards investing in these people and giving them some responsibility.
Honor creates access! Honor is the key to greater access to leadership. Here are some characteristics of dishonor towards leadership

that will diminish access and make it difficult for the leader to identify honor...

> Competing with your leader
> Speaking negatively of the leader
> Badmouthing your former organization
> Allowing others to vent negative feelings
> Not communicating consistently
> Ignoring opportunities
> Being absent

These are characteristics that are displayed regularly in Churches and organizations that make it difficult for a leader to entrust opportunity and responsibility to. Leaders tend to move away from people who display these characteristics. So great leaders identify not only skills and potential but also honor, not just for the leader himself but for the organization as a whole.

Honoring the vision versus honoring the leader. Some leaders are so over focused on those who honor them that they divert honor from the vision and the organization. Great companies have a mutual honor for the company and organization itself not just the leadership. Honor for the employees and the philosophy of the organization.

Just having honor for the leader without honoring the constituents and customers is detrimental to the organization. Every organization has a culture. That culture should be a culture of honor for the company and its mission and vision. Then it becomes about not just honoring what the leader does but honoring what we do as an organization. People have to have pride in what they are a part of believing that it is making a difference in the lives of people. Here are seven things we must honor about an organization...

> It's Mission
> It's Values
> It's History
> It's Culture
> It's People
> It's Customers
> It's Product or Service

Leaders who demand honor for themselves do the organization a disservice because they siphon the honor of the people from the rest of the organization.

Number 7 leaders don't give answers, they inspire pursuit. The worst thing that you can do as a leader is give people the answers. Giving people the answers to their problems isn't always the best way to lead. Rather inspire them to pursue their own answers. Inspire them to fall in love with wisdom and seek the answer to their problem.

It is the difference between giving someone a fish and teaching them to fish. One solves their problem for the moment until another one comes along. The latter equips them to solve their own problems for as long as they need to. Great leaders teach people how to think in a crisis. Great leaders teach people to ask the right questions in a crisis or any other situation.

These 7 leadership traits are not an exhaustive list by any means but they will help guide you as a leader and as a person under leadership to avoid the pitfalls of toxic leadership that so many have struggled with.

*Pray with me*

*Father thank you for the gift of leadership and for the amazing leaders that you have put in my life. Heal me from the residue of toxic leadership and help me to become the life giving leader that you desire for me to be in Jesus Name Amen!*

# Chapter Review and Key Points

- We often talk about the good qualities of leadership but fail to discuss the unsavory experiences that we have had with bad leadership. So the list above was inspired by my bad experiences with leadership that helped to shape me as a leader.

- Yes we have to check on people and feel out where they may be at but that is done subtly and with respect. It is called being political not in the bad sense but in the leadership sense. There are two kinds of people in this world those who initiate and those who react. We must learn to check on the people we care about and lead without seeming to violate their privacy.

- Great leaders don't spend their time always correcting their people but encouraging them. That may sound something like, "That is not something I would do", rather than, "that is a terrible decision". See the difference. Great leaders can correct you and make it feel like you have just been encouraged.

- Introverted leaders often find engaging with their people difficult. Introverted people often find disengagement easy. Introverted people tend to live in a state of disengagement instead of finding where they are naturally extroverted they never really discover where they engage with others most effectively.

- Honor must be identified not demanded. In other words who do you see that has genuine honor and respect for you and your gift? Once you identify honor in another you can begin to trust them more and more with leadership responsibility. Pour into those who show honor. Invest in those who show a hunger to learn and an interest in serving your vision.

## ಖ 3 ಲ

# The Orphan Spirit

One thing that is prevalent in today's society is what many call the orphan spirit. I worked in the foster care industry for some years and one thing that you would notice was that someone who did not grow up with parents but stayed in the foster care system became more difficult to parent and less likely to be adopted.

The longer they stayed in that system the more difficult it was for them to be adopted. They had developed the orphan attitude. They did not know how to be parented. They did not develop the trust and humility needed to be parented. It is the same in the Church today. Most people don't know how to be pastored or mentored and they certainly don't know how to be a protégé. They have developed the orphan spirit. An orphan spirit is an independent spirit that refuses to submit to any type of leadership. Here are seven characteristics of the orphan spirit...

> ➤ Cannot be trained
> ➤ Cannot receive correction
> ➤ Lacks interest and passion
> ➤ Displays no commitment
> ➤ Has no consistency
> ➤ Fragmented focus
> ➤ Takes no responsibility

These characteristics come from never having to serve anyone or anything. Those with the orphan spirit cannot be trained. Learning makes them feel less than instead of empowered. Those with an orphan spirit do not have a passion to learn and develop yet they always seem to feel broken and in need to be fixed.

They do not understand that they don't need to be fixed but they need to be invested into however any investment into their lives is a waste of time because they are bad soil. They will never be able to bring the seeds of leadership to harvest. The scripture says it best when it tells us in II Timothy 3:7 that, *"They are ever learning but never able to acknowledge the truth."*

They will not receive correction because it makes them feel uncomfortable. They are feeling oriented and correction brings them out of their comfort zone. They also lack passion and often show disinterest in the visions of supporting leadership. They lack commitment and don't understand the Psalm 1:3 principle that says, *"That person is like a tree planted by the rivers of water which yields it fruit in season and whose leaf does not whither, whatever they do shall prosper."*

Planted people prosper! The orphan spirit does not stay anywhere for long. As soon as they have to reveal who they really are they go to the next venue. They only stay long enough to paint a picture of who they want people to think they are. The orphan spirit is inconsistent and unable to stay focused.

They usually have what I call shiny object syndrome. They are initially excited at the beginning but when something else shinier comes along they switch focus to the new thing not ever finishing what they start. They refuse to develop the spirit of a finisher.

Finally they take no responsibility. They don't want to build or move towards ownership they only enjoy renting space in the lives of those around them. Rejection and lack of identity are the traits that those with an orphan spirit will have. People with these traits often display a victim mentality and blame everyone else for their problems.

Serving another qualifies you to lead and being faithful with someone else's will guarantee that you have your own one day. We see this in the life of David. Let's talk a little bit about being able to serve a leader and how that qualifies you for leadership in your own right.

One of my favorite passages in The Bible is II Samuel chapter 6. It is all about The Ark of The Covenant coming back into Jerusalem. Because believe it or not for the whole reign of King Saul The Ark was not in Israel but had been captured by the philistines.

So when David becomes King He decides to bring The Ark back into Jerusalem. The Ark was not God but represented God. The Ark was where The Kabowd (Kabod) or Glory of God rested between the Cherubs wings that were sculpted and covered in gold on tip of The Ark. It means the weight, splendor, glory, and abundance of God. Israel followed that Ark and put it at the front of their armies in battle.

Let's look at this passage so we can understand what The Ark is all about in II Samuel chapter 6: 1-22.

*1. David again brought together out of Israel chosen men, thirty thousand in all.*
*2 He and all his men set out from Baalah of Judah [1] to bring up from there the ark of God, which is called by the Name, [2] the name of the LORD Almighty, who is enthroned between the cherubim that are on the ark.*

So now we see The Ark and that God was enthroned between the cherubim on The Ark.
*3 They set the ark of God on a new cart and brought it from the house of Abinadab, which*

was on the hill. Uzzah and Ahio, sons of Abinadab, were guiding the new cart
4 with the ark of God on it, [3] and Ahio was walking in front of it.
    Now remember Ahio and Uzzah were the sons of Abinidab where The Ark had been. So they become too familiar with The Ark that they said we will guide it. Now last time I checked we don't guide God but He guides us. But when we become so familiar with the presence of God we think that we can tell God what to do. Also this needs to be noted.
    The Above scripture tells us that they set The Ark of God on a new cart. This is an interesting point because The Ark according to Leviticus law was only to be carried on the Priests shoulders with two poles that The Ark set on. So we can see already that their familiarity with the presence of God cause them to not follow the protocol of God's presence and instead they just threw it on a cart.
    First thing we need to understand is that you don't drag The Glory of God you carry it. It is very important to see the mistakes that they made because it explains God's anger.

5 David and the whole house of Israel were celebrating with all their might before the LORD, with songs [4] and with harps, lyres, tambourines, sistrums and cymbals.
6 When they came to the threshing floor of Nacon, Uzzah reached out and took hold of the ark of God, because the oxen stumbled.

This is where it all changes. Uzzah saw that the oxen stumbled and reached out and touched The Ark to steady it. God was angered by this and struck Uzzah dead. Why did God strike Uzzah dead? Because the law states in the book of Numbers that you cannot touch The Ark or you will die. They became so accustomed to having The Ark around that they forgot to show honor and obey the protocol.

They got lazy with the Glory. Let's skip down to verse 17. David got angry with God about killing Uzzah and said I don't want to bring The Ark into Jerusalem so he sent it to Obed-Edom's house and God started to bless Obed-Edom because of The Ark and David said Wait a minute if God is blessing him because of The Ark then I want it in Jerusalem with me. Verse thirteen tells us, *"13 When those who were carrying the ark of the LORD had taken six steps, he sacrificed a bull and a fattened calf."*

David goes and gets The Ark from Obed-Edom's house and this time he carries it on the poles set on the priest's shoulders. And the Bible says that every six steps they worshipped and sacrificed. So they went from throwing The Ark on the back of a cart to carrying it on the Priest's shoulders and sacrificing every six steps.

That sounds like a heart change to me. We've done exactly the same thing on the Church. We have seen so much of The Presence of God in our lives and God has grown our Churches and given us great success, however, we have become so familiar with God and so

excited about His blessing that we have removed the thing that got us there in the first place.
It was a heart of honor and the protocol of His presence. So today we hear shocking news of a mega Church pastor taking his own life nearly every few months in America. Why because we have forgotten God.
We have sold out to a system of Church and have what the Apostle Paul says is a form of godliness that denies the power. Another scripture that is important to look at is I Samuel 6 which tells us, *5 After the Philistines had captured the ark of God, they took it from Ebenezer to Ashdod. 2 Then they carried the ark into Dagon's temple and set it beside Dagon.3 When the people of Ashdod rose early the next day, there was Dagon, fallen on his face on the ground before the ark of the Lord! They took Dagon and put him back in his place. 4 But the following morning when they rose, there was Dagon, fallen on his face on the ground before the ark of the Lord! His head and hands had been broken off and were lying on the threshold; only his body remained.*
So I love this part. The Philistines took The Ark and placed it in their pagan temple of dagon. In the morning the dagon statue was bowed before The Ark. The next morning the dagon statues head and hands were broken off and it was bowed before The Ark, and God began to judge the Philistines. So the Philistines ask their pagan priest to send The Ark back to the

Israelites and the priests had this wisdom. **6** When the ark of the Lord had been in Philistine territory seven months, **2** the Philistines called for the priests and the diviners and said, "What shall we do with the ark of the Lord? Tell us how we should send it back to its place."

**3** They answered, "If you return the ark of the god of Israel, do not send it back to him without a gift; by all means send a guilt offering to him. Then you will be healed, and you will know why his hand has not been lifted from you."

Now this is interesting to me. The Philistine priests said "Don't just send it back send it back with an offering of gold. What did they just say? If you send it back with an offering of gold then their God will heal us.

So how is it that a pagan culture and pagan priests know how to show honor and have more fear of God that even God's own people. We read earlier that David and his men threw The Ark on the back of a cart and started dragging it instead of carrying it, but the pagan priests send it back with a guilt offering of gold.

It is stunning how familiar we can become with God that we lose our fear of God. The fear of God is so important that it impacts our lives and affects the way we carry ourselves and what we place value on.

The Bible tells us that the fear of The Lord is the beginning of wisdom. Yes God is loving and yes God is gracious more than we even know or recognize. But even a child know don't play so long on the floor with your daddy that you forget that He's your daddy. The fear of The Lord is not being afraid but having such a sense of honor and reverence that you are afraid to disobey God.

It is a fear born out of respect that you're not dealing with a normal person here but The Living God. They had become so comfortable with God that they forgot His laws and His ways. You'll never get so comfortable with God that He will change his rules and protocol for you. That is exactly what the Church has done. Become to acquainted with Grace that we have forgotten the fear of The Lord and though His Favor is in His right hand His judgment is in His other hand.

So what does all this Ark teaching have to do with Church anyways? I'm glad you asked. I have one more scripture that I want us to look at in Jeremiah 3:15-16. It tells us, *15 And I will give you pastors according to mine heart, which shall feed you with knowledge and understanding.*

*16 And it shall come to pass, when ye be multiplied and increased in the land, in those days, saith the Lord, they shall say no more, The ark of the covenant of the Lord: neither shall it come to mind: neither shall they remember it; neither shall they visit it; neither shall that be done any more.*

Wow did you read that? This scripture tells us that the people will no longer follow The

Ark or ask about it but God will give them Pastors according to His heart. Now you will no longer follow a gold covered box but you will follow my pastors or leaders that will give you knowledge and understanding.

So if there is no longer an Ark but now God has given us pastors we must deduce that whatever God put in The Ark He now will put in His leaders. The Ark had Aaron's rod that budded, the Jar of Manna, and the Ten Commandments. The Ten Commandments are the Message, Aaron's Rod or Staff that Budded was the Mantle, and The Jar of Manna was the Miracle.

The Message, the Mantle, and the Miracle needed a new resting place and God decide to put them in His leaders, His pastors. That's right your pastor is now The Ark of God. Pastors are carriers of God's presence and they hold in them the Message, the Mantle, and the Miracle of God. Not because of who they are but because of who God is in them.

No longer will a golden box lead God's people but men full of The Holy Ghost and power. So the next time you look at your pastor don't see a hired hand that preaches a good sermon. See Him as God sees him as an Ark of God's presence that possess a message, mantle, and miracle for you and your family.

We have replaced The Ark in our Churches with hirelings, motivational speakers, and life coaches. There is nothing wrong with motivational speakers and life coaches it's just they don't belong on the Altar of God and they don't possess God's Message, His Mantle, or His Miracle. God is raising up a generation of Kingdom Leaders, Pastors, and Apostles that carry the Message, Mantle, and Miracle of God so that God's people can once again experience His Glory.

So let's take it a step further. Do we treat our pastor like an Ark or like a mere man? Remember Uzzah stretched his hand out and touched The Ark. How many of us touch our leader or try to tell him how it should be done? If the pastor is an Ark he should be honored like The Ark. Are you guiding him or are you letting Him guide you and train you? Seven attitudes that unlock the Message, Mantle, and Miracle in your pastor...

➢ Be Teachable
➢ Be Humble
➢ Be Generous
➢ Be Expectant
➢ Show Honor
➢ Be available to Serve
➢ Be Present

Some would argue with me that pastors are just men and we shouldn't put them on a pedestal. Well you put celebrities on pedestals and athletes on pedestals and they don't carry the Message, Mantle, or Miracle. God has elevated your Pastor, Bishop, or Apostle. They are already on a pedestal and you didn't put them there, God did. You just have to recognize it and change your perspective. God has chosen men to reveal Himself through and that was not our choice but his. Men are flawed and fallible but even David would not touch Saul when He has the opportunity to kill him. Because He would not touch God's Anointed. Even though Saul had an evil spirit and was not serving God he was still Anointed King. And David honored him and God honored David for it. Your Pastor's flaws and weaknesses don't disqualify him from your respect and honor. He has a position in God and as The Ark was to be carried so you Pastor, Bishop, Apostle needs to be carried held up in prayer and support by showing honor.

The Bible says he who receives a prophet in the name of a prophet will receive a prophet's reward. If you perceive you will receive. What do I mean? Simple, I must first perceive you as a prophet before I can receive the prophet's reward. How do you perceive your pastor? As a hired hand that can be replaced if you don't like what he is doing and saying, or God's man for the hour in your Church who possesses a Mantle, Message, and Miracle that will bless your family.

*Pray with me*

*Father thank you for giving me a heart of leadership and if there are any characteristics of the orphan spirit in my life help me to be healed of any wounds from toxic leadership in my past and move forward in my leadership journey Jesus Name Amen!*

# Chapter Review and Key Points

- Those with the orphan spirit cannot be trained. Learning makes them feel less than instead of empowered. Those with an orphan spirit do not have a passion to learn and develop yet they always seem to feel broken and in need to be fixed.

- Planted people prosper! The orphan spirit does not stay anywhere for long. As soon as they have to reveal who they really are they go to the next venue. They only stay long enough to paint a picture of who they want people to think they are. The orphan spirit is inconsistent and unable to stay focused.

- No longer will a golden box lead God's people but men full of The Holy Ghost and power. So the next time you look at your pastor don't see a hired hand that preaches a good sermon. See Him as God sees him as an Ark of God's presence that possess a message, mantle, and miracle for you and your family.

- You just have to recognize it and change your perspective. God has chosen men to reveal Himself through and that was not our choice but his. Men are flawed and fallible but even David would not touch Saul when He has the opportunity to kill him.

## ⁂ 4 ⁂

# Father's Help You Finish

~~~~~

There is a disconnect today related to leadership and mentorship. Mentorship is necessary for success and many leaders today refuse to engage in mentorship because of the personal investment of time that it requires.

Just because someone is a leader does not mean that they are equipped to mentor you. Mentorship is another level of leadership. A mentor is more like a father figure. They have been where you're going and made the mistakes that you have yet to make.

In a famous passage in I Corinthians 4:15 the Apostle Paul says, *"Even if you had ten thousand teachers in Christ, you do not have many fathers, for in Christ Jesus I became your father through the Gospel."*

The Apostle Paul is distinguishing the difference here between a teacher and a father. Fathers are the most uncelebrated roles in the earth today but the most important. Mother's Day is third on the list of most money spent on Holiday's behind Christmas and Easter.

Father's Day is like not even top ten. It is popular to raise children today without a father in the home in fact it is rewarded by the government and the court systems. Our society has slowly pushed fathers out of their roles, on TV and in real life.

You cannot push someone out of their roles and then accuse them of not being there. Mothers and children will be real quick in today's society to disparage a father or not respect his role in the family or the children's lives at the same time be very quick in accusing him of not being there or abandoning them.

This could not be further from the truth. Pushing a leader or a father out of his roles and then accusing him of not being there is very hypocritical. Either a father deserves the respect that he should get and you are submitted to that or remove yourself from his covering. But you cannot have it both ways.

If you have fully submitted to a father or leader and he abuses that power or abandons you then you have the right to say that he was not there. But if he tried to be the best father and leader that he could be and you made that job super difficult, disrespected him and forced him out of his role as father and leader then you have no right to accuse him of not being there. You did that to yourself honey! Men get a bad rap in society today because they are the ones that are quickly blamed for not being there even when their presence was not wanted or honored. You cannot block a leader or father from doing his job and then accuse him of not doing his job. Here are seven things that father's do both spiritual and biological...

➢ Bring Identity DNA
➢ Assign Value
➢ Make a Deposit
➢ Connect you to Resource
➢ Link you to your Future
➢ Let you make Mistakes
➢ Teach you Honor

First Father's bring identity. You carry your father's last name. There is a genealogy of knowing who you are that comes from your father. Adam the first man was given an assignment from God. It is found in Genesis 2:19-20 and it tells us, *"Now the Lord God had formed out of the ground all the wild animals and all the birds in the sky. He brought them to the man to see what he would name them, and whatever the man called each living creature, that was its name. So the man gave names to all the livestock, the birds in the sky and all the wild animals."* There is an interesting phrase in that passage that says, *"...whatever the man called each living creature that was its name."* When God wanted to name the animals that he just created he didn't take them to the woman she was not even created yet. God gave the responsibility for identity to the MAN.

Men bring identity. Father's show you who you are. The words of a Father are very powerful. You become whatever a father calls you. That is why fathers must be careful not to call their children words like stupid or derogatory phrases because it IMPRINTS on the psyche and the spirit of the child.

To whom much is given much is required. The power of identity is a big responsibility and people will often live up to the words of their father whether good or bad. Fathers also bring identity through their DNA. DNA is the written code of information passed down from the father, which carries his traits both good and bad.

Have you ever heard someone say, you remind me of your father? This is true in the spiritual realm as well. A mentor or father will pass down gifts and impartation to protégés sons and spiritual daughters. I call it spiritual DNA. That is why the Father in Heaven sent his Son Jesus to shed his blood on the cross.

Not just to please the Father with the perfect sacrifice but to reintroduce the divine DNA that was missing from our bloodline that Adam lost when he sinned. I wrote an entire book called "Unlocking the Seven Secrets of the Blood", that explains this in more detail. Genetic material is passed down through the blood and spiritual material is passed down through the spiritual bloodline as well. That is why everyone should have a mentor or spiritual father. Something will be missing from your identity if you skip that part of your life. Fathers prepare you for what is to come. The son that is just a boy wants to put shaving cream on his face while he watches his father shave. Why? Because he is looking at his future!

Number two Father's assign value. We have a generation of kids that don't know their worth and value because they never had a father who showed them. The daughter that has daddy issues that sleeps with every man that shows her any attention has never had a father show her worth and value.

If I lose a pencil I can just buy another pencil but if I lose my grandfather's gold watch I cannot replace that. God creates wealth! Anything God create has incredible value. Wealth is not something that you have wealth is who you are! God didn't replace us He redeemed us. He came to get us because we were too valuable to just replace.

Many people have thrown antiques in the attic only to discover later that its value was priceless at a local auction. It took a skilled appraiser to dust the family heirloom off and be able to assess its true value. Some of you have assessed your value by the opinions of unskilled and uncertified people. An appraiser is able to trace the heirloom back to its original creator and assess its true value based upon its uniqueness.

You need to get around some certified appraisers that can lead you back to your creator, God, and assess your value through His eyes and original intent. Father's and mentors can accurately assess your value.

Value is determined by the highest bidder. In the antiques world the value is determined by what people are willing to pay for it. So to know your own worth you have to assess that by the highest bidder.

Well, two thousand years ago Jesus of Nazareth paid the highest price for humanity when He hung on a Cross and died for our sins. He paid the highest price for you so that you would know how valuable you are. You were worth the blood of God's Son. You were bought with a price that no one else but God could pay.

So now you are what God says you are. Your value cannot be assessed by random people because people are not certified appraisers. Only God is! God has handpicked spiritual father's and mentors to assess your value properly and unlock the full potential of your life.

Next spiritual fathers make a deposit. Jesus said the Words that I speak to you are Spirit and Life. Those leaders that God has placed in your life make a deposit of the seed of God into your life.

The seed of God is growing while you are sleeping. The seed of the Kingdom of God is working in you while you are not even aware of what's happening. As you continue to feed your faith with the Word and water it with the presence of God, new mercy and grace will spring up every day.

Seeds may lie dormant but they don't die. They just spring up the next season that comes around. The grass might turn brown and look like it is dead but it's not dead it's just dormant and when the sun starts shining and the rains start falling the seed wakes up again and starts to grow.

I came here to tell someone that the seed of God inside of you is not dead it is just lying dormant because of what you went through and because of some of the decisions that you made, but every dormant seed comes alive in a new season. The things that you thought were dead are coming to life again and waking up. New mercy and new favor are overtaking your life because the dormant seeds have been awakened by the Word of God. Some seeds spring up suddenly.

Next fathers connect you to resource. Father means SOURCE. In other words fathers are life source relationships. Jesus talked to the woman at the well who was arguing with him about wells. She was going to resource when Jesus offered her source. Let's look at this scripture found in John 4:7, *"7 When a Samaritan woman came to draw water, Jesus said to her, "Will you give me a drink?" 8 His disciples had gone into the town to buy food. 9 The Samaritan woman said to him, "You are a*

*Jew and I am a Samaritan woman. How can you ask me for a drink?" 10 Jesus answered her, "If you knew the gift of God and who it is that asks you for a drink, you would've asked him and he would've given you living water."*

Jesus basically said to this woman this well is a resource and it will run out. But I am a source, and source never runs out. The world is running to resource and resource is bound to run dry but source never runs dry. God is our source and his supply is limitless. A Father or mentor on your life who represents God's delegated authority is a life source that will always have a fresh word for you. That must be honored and celebrated. I can't tell you times where I needed a word from God and I had prayed and prayed and my mentor was teaching and as I listened to his teaching God spoke to me and answered a question that I had been asking for years.

I asked God why didn't you just tell me. He said if I tell you everything then what is the purpose of mentorship. There are some things that God will only tell you through the agency of another person. Father's and mentors always connect you to the source, which is God Himself. God has a delegated chain of command and if you cannot hear from someone you can see, how can you ever learn from a God you cannot see?

Next fathers link you to your future. The enemy is not fighting what you are doing, he is fighting who you are becoming. There is power in becoming. You cannot be what you are not but you can become what you're not. I cannot be great but I can become great.

Father's help you become what you are not. The only difference between who you are now and next year will be what you learn. Wisdom changes you into another person. Many are aware of how much a child needs a father, but few are aware of how much a grown adult needs a father or mentor in their lives. Now is the seed for next and a father will show you how to invest in your now in order to create your next. Everybody talks about "One Day". One day I'll be rich. One day I'll be smart enough. One day I'll be gifted enough. One day is never coming. Today is here and I can use my TODAY to create my tomorrow. It is called investment. A father shows you how to invest in your present to create your future.

Here are seven things you can invest in right now...

- ➢ Invest Time
- ➢ Invest Wisdom
- ➢ Invest Money
- ➢ Invest Gifts
- ➢ Invest Love
- ➢ Invest Ideas
- ➢ Invest Words

Fathers invest all of these into your life! A spiritual father will invest quality time into your life as well as the wisdom that he has excavated throughout his life. A father will often invest money into your dreams and impart gifts to your life. Fathers also invest love and ideas and finally words that will become the self portrait that you live by.

We do not live what we know, we live who we believe. Someday you'll believe someone and that day will determine the rest of your life. That is the importance of a spiritual father or mentor.

Next fathers let you make mistakes. Fathers never tell you what to do but they will always help you to learn from their mistakes. Father's will show you the power of a mistake because that will turn you into the best mentor for those you are leading. I heard one lady who is now a CEO of a fortune 500 company say, *"When I was a kid my dad would sit at the dinner table and ask us kids where we failed today. We would say that we failed at this or that. I would say I tried out for the basketball team and didn't make it. He would say, that is great sweetie you tried. We did that for so many years that failure wasn't a bad thing to me. When I failed I saw it as an opportunity to learn and now I take that same mentality into my career as a CEO."*

What an amazing thought that her father allowed her to fail and even celebrated it. Father's help you take failures and extract the wisdom from it. I had a similar experience in graduate school. I took a speaking class and the first day of class the professor asked one of us to

get up in front of the class and read a scripture. It was actually a preaching class. I had been preaching already for years so I thought I was big stuff. I got up and arrogantly read the scripture to the class and sat down. My professor proceeded to ask the class to raise their hand and tell the class what they thought I did wrong and the professor wrote each one up on the board.
 Now initially I was embarrassed but I never learned more from a moment than that. I learned I wasn't as great as I thought I was. I ended up making a 96 in that class and all of my speaking opportunities that I had in the class were amazing. That professor became a mentor to me and since I have traveled all over the world speaking to thousands of audiences and crowds all because I chose to celebrate my mistakes. My mentor allowed me to make the mistakes and helped me become better!
 Finally fathers teach you honor! You can watch a mother with her children as they recklessly trounce around the mall ignoring her every command. Then all of a sudden a deep assertive voice bellows through the noise and everyone stops. There is something about a father's voice that gets the kids attention.
 Fathers can get a child in line with only a glance in their direction. Fathers are built by God to teach honor and respect. Honor is the willingness celebrate someone's difference. Honor unlocks doors of favor. I am convinced we have a generation of unruly adults because of

fatherless homes and the inability of single mothers to teach their children how to honor.

The very last verse of the Old Testament found in Malachi 4:5 goes something like this, *"5 See, I will send the prophet Elijah to you before that great and dreadful day of the Lord comes. 6 He will turn the hearts of the children to their father's and the hearts of their fathers to their children, or else I will come and strike the land with a curse."*

This verse is the last verse of the Old Testament in the Bible. Now last sayings are very important and this is the last thing God is saying before he goes silent for 400 years. So what does he say? He says if fathers are not put back into the proper place in society I will curse the land. That word for curse means to destroy. God is saying that the absence of fatherhood in the lives of people is causing destruction and that needs to change.

Without father's we don't know who to honor. Spiritual fathers teach is how to honor God. Mentors and fathers train us to honor God in all our ways so that we can finish the race and complete our assignment. Here are seven things spiritual fathers help you to honor…

- The Laws of God
- The Wisdom of God
- The Order of God
- The Value of Favor
- The Word of God

- The Vessel of God
- The Investment of God

Fathers help you finish. One of my favorite videos is about a young man who was qualifying for the Olympics. This was his final race to qualify for the Olympic games. The gun sounds and they're off. The runners get about halfway around the track and suddenly the young man buckles in pain and falls down. The crowd gasps as they see him get up and begin limping around the track in obvious pain with tears streaming down his face. A race that he has prepared for his whole life was now lost and he was still determined to finish with a limp but the emotion and pain seemed too strong.

Out of nowhere the camera pans towards the crowd and you see heavy set man pushing through security and making his way out onto the track ignoring all instructions to go back to his seat. He makes his way to the track and runs after his son meeting him on the track as he is limping and weeping. The father looks at his son and says, "Let's finish this together."

Grabbing his son by the arm and placing his other arm around his lower back the father walks with his son as they make it around the track and finish the race together. The young man was weeping and burying his head in his father's shoulder. They crossed the finish line together. Without his father he would've struggled to finish the race, but his father found him in a painful situation and helped him finish what he started. That is what a spiritual father or mentor will do for you. When you feel like you cannot go on any longer they meet you at your place of pain and walk with you to the finish line. Fathers help you finish! Why?

Because that is what our Heavenly Father does for us. He helps us finish by putting powerful mentors and fathers in our lives to take us on to the finish line. Who is a mentor in your life? Who is helping you get there even when it hurts? Who is encouraging you not to quit? That is who you should honor as a father and mentor.

*Pray with me*

*Father thank you for mentors and fathers that you have placed in my life who have trained me and helped to develop my passion and gifting. Help me to honor them in Jesus Name Amen!*

# Chapter Review and Key Points

- There is a lot being said about vision today but everyone wants their own vision and no one seems to want to serve the vision of another. Vision seems to be the flavor of the month currently and we are in danger of building our own empires instead of building God's vision for our life.

- You may be thinking well I thought that a vision from God would feel amazing and that it would bring me great peace? Ask Jonah when God gave him a vision to go to Nineveh and preach. He ran the other way. Ask Saul when Jesus knocked him off of his horse and called him to minister to the Gentiles. I'm sure these God-given callings were somewhat uncomfortable.

- Don't shy away from the responsibility that God has given you. You can't just serve when you feel like it. You can't just serve when it feels good. You have to serve when you don't feel like it and when it is not as successful as you think that it should be.

- The call of God feels weighty and it comes with great authority. The call to serve God and his house are no small thing. This is BIG! Many times we shy away from the call of God because we do not want to be responsible for people. We like our little life that we have built and we don't want to meddle in other people's business.

## ༄ 5 ༅

# The Pursuit

The most important thing that you can learn about leadership and mentorship as well as spiritual covering is that it is not the mentor's job to pursue the protégé. It is not the leader's job to chase the follower down. It is not the teacher's job to chase the student. The pursuit is on the protégés side.

We live in a society where everything is obtained at the push of a button. So we have become very self serving. You don't even have to get off the couch to order anything you want whether food or facial cream. All you have to do is push a button. So the idea that you have to actually get up and go after something has been greatly trivialized due to the advances of the

Internet and smart phones. So we have adopted the idea that if I'm supposed to have it it'll just come to me. Well, that is not how life works. Life doesn't happen to you. Life responds to you! Life responds to what you put out there. To the seed that you sow. To the efforts and engagement that you create.

Mentorship and leadership works the same way. As the late president JFK once said, "Ask not what your country can do for you, ask rather what you can do for your country." In other words what problem can you solve? What can you offer to the situation to make it better? Who have you helped today? Mentorship works the same way.

If you see a future that you desire, you have to go after it. Someone who has something that you don't have knows something that you don't know. Let the pursuit begin. Find someone who has what you want or is doing what you want to do and sit at their feet and learn. Don't go after their stuff go after their wisdom. The biggest mistake that people make when pursuing a mentor or spiritual father is to want what they have instead of wanting to know what they know.

I'm amazed at people who tell me they are starting a business and I ask them who is mentoring them in that area and they respond with, "No one". Really are you serious? You are going to just wing it? It will take you ten times as long to make the mistakes and learn from them than to just learn from the mistakes of a mentor and get a head start. But time and time again people choose the long way around. Mentorship and spiritual fathering have much more to do with impartation than information. There is a transfer of leadership of spiritual DNA.

One of the most powerful men in the Bible was Elisha. The Elijah Elisha relationship is that of a mentoring and fathering one. Let's look closer at this passage to see how it applies to us today.

In I King 19:19 we read, *"19 So Elijah went from there and found Elisha son of Shaphat. He was plowing with twelve yoke of oxen, and he himself was driving the twelfth pair. Elijah went up to him and threw his cloak around him. 20 Elisha then left his oxen and ran after Elijah. "Let me kiss my father and mother goodbye he said", "And then I will come with you." "Go back", Elijah replied, "What have I done to you?" 21 So Elisha left him and went back. He took his yoke of oxen and slaughtered them. He burned the plowing equipment to cook the meat and gave it to the people and they ate. Then he set out to follow Elijah and became his servant."*

I love this passage because it show the power of pursuit. Notice Elijah didn't wait to be called on he ran after Elijah it tells us in the scripture. The pursuit was on the protégé. The mentor simply made the connection but the protégé was the one that had to begin the pursuit. A great person is not going to chase you down. Your mentor is not going to run after you and beg you to follow. There must be a pursuit on your part. Mentorship must be pursued by the protégé and if your passion to learn doesn't push you to pursue a mentor then you aren't really serious. Here are seven ways to pursue a mentor...

> Ask a question
> Get involved
> Start to serve
> Solve a problem
> Lighten his load
> Offer your support
> Study their life

    Elisha didn't wait for seventeen confirmations, he simply stated to pursue. You don't love what you say you love. You love what you pursue. The passion is in the pursuit. You can say you love someone but if you do not pursue them it is just words. True passion requires the chase the pursuit. Do you want it bad enough?
    Now Elisha ran into some resistance. We read where Elijah said, *"What did I do? Go back"*. Sometimes the mentor will seem like he has no time or interest to test the passion of the protégé. Don't take no for an answer. Elijah was testing the young prophet to see if he was serious. Elisha to show is commitment does something drastic. He burns his plow and kills his oxen. Now wait a minute. That seems kind

of extreme. Elisha did not just burn his plow he built an altar and sacrificed his oxen to God. Number one he sowed his business. Those oxen were his livelihood that brought in income for he and his family. He was willing to sacrifice and sow a BIG seed to show God that he was serious about mentorship and the Anointing of the Holy Spirit. First he burns his plow meaning that he didn't give himself anything to go back to. When you have nothing to return to you are less likely to attempt to quit your current pursuit and leave your current focus when things get tough. Some of you have a backup plan just in case your pursuit doesn't work out. Elisha burned his backup plan.

Following God and serving greatness requires sacrifice. Elijah was willing to sow a big seed and leave himself nothing to go back to show God and Elijah that he was serious about his future. Elijah did three things that qualified him for mentorship...

> He pursued vs. 20
> He sacrificed vs. 21
> He partnered vs. 21

I've already established that pursuit is proof of passion. Not only did Elisha pursue Elijah his mentor and spiritual father but he even pursued him when Elijah himself pushed the young protégé away. One of my favorite passages of scripture is found in II Kings chapter 2. It reads, *"And it came to pass when the Lord would take up Elijah into heaven by a whirlwind that Elisha went with Elijah from Gilgal. 2 And Elijah said unto Elisha, Tarry here I pray thee for the Lord hath sent me to Bethel. And Elisha said unto him, "AS the Lord lives and as they soul lives I will not leave thee. So they went down to Bethel. 3 And the sons of the prophets that where at Bethel came forth to Elisha and said unto him, "Know thou that the Lord will take away the master from thy head today?" And he said, "Yea I know it, hold your peace. 4 And Elijah said unto him, Elisha, tarry here I pray thee for the Lord hath sent me to Jericho. And he said, "As the Lord lives and as thy soul lives I will not leave you. So they came to Jericho. 5 And the sons of the prophets that were at Jericho came to Elisha and said unto him know you not that the Lord will take away your master from your head today?" And he answered yea I know it. Hold your peace. 6 And Elijah said unto him Tarry I pray thee here for the Lord has sent me to Jordan. And he said to him as the Lord lives and as your soul lives I will not leave you. And they two went on. 7 And fifty men of the sons of the prophets went and stood to view afar off and they two stood by the Jordan. 8 Elijah took his mantle and wrapped together and smote the waters and they were divided here and there so that they two went over on dry ground. 9 And it came to pass when they were gone over that Elijah said unto Elisha ask what I shall do for thee before I be taken away from thee. And Elisha* said, "I pray thee let a double portion of thy spirit be upon me. 10 and it came to pass as they still went on and talked that behold there appeared a chariot of fire and horses of fire and parted them both asunder, and Elijah went up by a whirlwind into heaven. 12 And Elisha saw it and he cried out, "My father my father the chariot of Israel and the horsemen thereof. And he saw him no more and he took hold of his own clothes and tore them in two pieces. 13 He took up also the mantle of Elijah that fell from him and went back and stood by the bank of the Jordan. 14 And he took the mantle of Elijah that fell from him and smote the waters and said, "Where is the Lord God od Elijah?" And when he also had smitten the waters they parted here and there and Elisha went over."

It is interesting that Elijah when he was preparing to go to the next city told his young protégé to stay back. Was this a test or did he really intend to move on without him? It seems that he was testing his resolve and how hungry Elisha was for the mantle of Elijah.

The four cities that Elijah went to are somewhat of a picture of the seasons of fathering that we will go through to qualify for greater levels of Anointing in our life and ministry. First he went to Gilgal. Gilgal was the place of decision. It means "Wheel". Gilgal is the place where things begin and the ball gets rolling so to speak. Elisha made a decision to follow at Gilgal.

This is the season in your life where you start out on this mentorship journey and things are very new. You begin to learn the values of your man of God or mentor and you start to learn his protocol for things. Gilgal is the first city that Israel camped in after they crossed the Jordan. This might be your first experience with a spiritual covering and here is what you can expect...

➤ To feel the weight of greatness
➤ To see the human side of a mentor
➤ To sow seeds of honor
➤ To see competition among protégés
➤ To be corrected
➤ To be scrutinized
➤ To be criticized

As Elisha was following Elijah on this journey the sons of the prophets often taunted and reeled at Elisha. Your journey will be met with people who are jealous of your pursuit. Even people who believe just like you will attack you for no reason. Keep your focus! Elisha told the sons of the prophets to hold their peace.
Translation, "Be quiet!" There will be haters on this journey but they didn't get the mantle, Elisha did! The mantle doesn't go to the ones who want it, it goes to the one who pursues it, serves it, and sows into it!
The next city Elijah went to was Bethel. Bethel means house of God. Bethel is the place of commitment. Where you lock in and say I will

put God's house first in my life. David was the second King of Israel and a man after God's own heart. Acts 13:34 tells us that God gave to us through Christ the sure mercies of David. Why did God love David so much? There is a reason and the Bible calls it the "Sure mercies of David". God favored King David more than any other person in the Bible other than Jesus. He allowed Solomon to build the Temple because of the mercies of David. David loved the House of God!

God favored David because David said my eyes shall know no rest until I build the House of the Lord. He also said in Psalm 122:1, *"I was glad when they said unto me let us go unto the House of The Lord."* David loved the house of God so much that God favored him in a special way. Even in the second coming of Christ he will sit on the throne of David. God loves those who love his House and Elisha made a point to commit to the house of God at Bethel.

The third place that Elijah went to was Jericho. Now Jericho was a place of battle and represents a season of warfare. Before you receive any mantle of leadership and Anointing you will go through some battles. Here are the five battles that will precede you receiving the Mantle of the Kingdom...

> ➢ Battle over your Faith
> ➢ Battle over your Family
> ➢ Battle over your Favor
> ➢ Battle over your Finances

> Battle over your Future

Battle is the seed for peace! Battle is the seed for territory. If you got what you got without a fight then the devil didn't mind you having it. Every great breakthrough is preceded by a battle. You will go through mind battles regarding your mentor or spiritual father. Is this journey worth it? Questions like this will fill your mind. Your finances and family may be attacked spiritually. You may have seasons of depression.

But once you make it through the battle season you only have one season left and that it the Jordan. When Elijah arrived at the Jordan he asked Elisha, "What do you want?" Elisha said I want a double portion of your spirit. When you enter the Jordan season of your life you can ask for what you want and God will give it to you.

It is the season where your dreams become reality and you have learned valuable lessons from your mentor and now God is going to give you your own! You will be released into a season of favor and blessing because you endured your preparation. Mentors don't come into your life for your past but for your future.

Elisha knew the secret of pursuit! He knew the secret of God's divine chain of command and he pursued it with passion. He went through the four seasons of preparation and you will too...

- Gilgal season (Pursuit)
- Bethel season (Commit)
- Jericho season (Battle)
- Jordan season (Mantle)

Don't ever make a mentor chase you down. A true father in the faith will never pursue you but you must pursue them. The rewards of mentorship and spiritual covering will be eternal.

*Pray with me*
*Father I desire to be under the proper spiritual covering in my life. Help me to discern the voice that will usher me into my promise and unlock my future in Jesus Name!*

## Chapter Review and Key Points

- Mentorship and leadership works the same way. As the late president JFK once said, "Ask not what your country can do for you, ask rather what you can do for your country." In other words what problem can you solve? What can you offer to the situation to make it better? Who have you helped today? Mentorship works the same way.

- Elisha didn't wait for seventeen confirmations, he simply stated to pursue. You don't love what you say you love. You love what you pursue. The passion is in the pursuit. You can say you love someone but if you do not pursue them it is just words. True passion requires the chase the pursuit. Do you want it bad enough?

- He was willing to sacrifice and sow a BIG seed to show God that he was serious about mentorship and the Anointing of the Holy Spirit. First he burns his plow meaning that he didn't give himself anything to go back to. When you have nothing to return to you are less likely to attempt to quit your current pursuit and leave your current focus.

- As Elisha was following Elijah on this journey the sons of the prophets often taunted and reeled at Elisha. Your journey will be met with people who are jealous of your pursuit. Even people who believe just like you will attack you for no reason. Keep your focus! Elisha told the sons of the prophets to hold their peace.

## ∞ 6 ∞

# The Divine Equation of Wealth

If I told you that there was an equation for creating wealth God's way and it required the addition of another person to your life, would you believe it?  We established in the first chapter that God doesn't give you money but that He gives you the ability to produce it or create it.

II Chronicles 20:20 tell us what that equation is and how it works in our lives.  It says, *"Believe in the Lord your God, so shall you be established.  Believe His prophets, so shall you prosper."*

This is an interesting verse because it says that believing God will establish you or the Hebrew word is support you.  Then it says to believe His prophets and prosper.  So your prosperity is not linked directly to God but to trusting or believing in His servant. There is a third component to the prosperity equation and it is a man of God.

In the original test it reads, support God and you will be supported or upheld, support His prophets and you will prosper. God will require you to trust His representative. God will require you to follow a man of God.

Now I know that some of you want to stop reading here. You're thinking oh another preacher that wants my money. Remember God is not trying to get something from you He is trying to get something to you, but He will require you to believe a man of God.

Millions around the world trust in Christ but remain broke, why? Because they sneer at His servants. If you cannot trust a man of God you can see, how can you trust a God who you cannot see? God put His blessing on a man called Abraham and said, *"Whoever blesses you I will bless."*

In other words God said to Abraham in Genesis 12 that whoever is good to you I will be good to them. God puts His blessing on people and when you like who God likes, God begins to move in your direction.

The key to your financial future is a man of God. There is no logical explanation for it. God is logical but mysterious. You cannot figure Him out and once you do you have stopped following God and now created a false God in your mind.

I'm not taking here about a financial mentor. I have other books you can read about that. I am talking about a financial deliverer. There is a difference. Mentors are key in shaping your financial future but a man of God is a financial deliverer. Prosperity is more than money. Jacob didn't wrestle with God all night so that he could have some money. He already had that. Jacob didn't trick his brother out of his birthright so that he could have some money. Jacob didn't deceive his father into blessing him even though he was the younger so that he could have some more money.

No, he did these things because he wanted the blessing. The blessing is more than money. The blessing is the empowerment and endowment of God to be empowered to prosper.

What you want is the blessing the impartation of God's favor on your life that causes everything you touch to prosper. This only comes through connecting with someone that God has already blessed.

You are blessed through connection. Not just connection to God but connection to His representatives. Despising the servants of God is the key to poverty in your life. Bless a blessed man and God will bless you. This is the formula that brings prosperity and increase on your life. Here seven ways to connect with a blessed man...

> ➢ Absorb his wisdom

- Follow his instructions
- Sow into his Anointing
- Serve his purpose
- Seek his mentorship
- Stay close to him
- Celebrate his difference

First you must absorb his wisdom. What do I mean by this? Soak up his wisdom like a sponge. Read his books and listen to his teaching and make it the focus of your listening. Make him the most important voice in your life.

You must believe that when a man of God speaks it is as if God is speaking directly to you. Jesus said the words that I speak to you are spirit and life. This is not just information but impartation.

You are catching the essence of God's favor being released through a man of God's words. Some things are caught and some things are taught. You will catch some things that are intangible just like you will be taught some practical things from a man of God.

You have to become a protégé. A protégé is a skilled learner. Your future is in someone else's mouth. When a man of God that is assigned to you speaks your spirit will leap with faith and you will begin to believe God like never before.

Wisdom is the key to wealth. If you increase your wisdom you will increase your wealth. Solomon the famous King of Israel and the wisest man that ever lived asked God for wisdom and God gave him wealth and fame as well. Let's look at this scripture in II Chronicles 1:6-11. It says, *"6 Solomon went up to the bronze altar before the Lord in the tent of meeting and offered a thousand burnt offerings on it. 7 That night God appeared to Solomon and said to him, "Ask for whatever you want me to give you." 8 Solomon answered God, "You have shown great kindness to David my father and have made me King in his place. 9 Now Lord God let your promise to my father David be confirmed, for you have made me King over a people who are as numerous as the dust of the earth. 10 Give me wisdom and knowledge that I may lead this people, for who us able to govern this great people of yours?" 11 God said to Solomon, "Since this is your heart's desire and you have not asked for wealth, possessions or honor, nor for the death of your enemies, and since you have not asked for a long life but for wisdom and knowledge to govern my people over whom I have made you King, 12 therefore wisdom and knowledge will be given you. And I will also give you wealth, possessions and honor, such as no king who was before you ever had and none after you will have."*

    God basically said to Solomon you can have whatever you want and Solomon asked for the factor instead of the product. Wisdom is that factory for favor.

    First thing we read is that Solomon did was honor leadership. He addressed the people and called out the leaders of the nation. He said in verse 2, *"Then Solomon spoke to all Israel, to the commanders of thousands and commanders of hundreds, to the judges and to all the leaders in Israel, the heads of families."* Solomon addressed the leaders and in addressing the leaders he was addressing the nation, because the leaders would pass the information down the chain of command. Solomon also honored his father King David and offered 1000 burnt offerings on the Altar that Moses had made. The first step to prosperity is to acknowledge those who have gone before you. To honor your leaders and your parents is vital to prosperity.

Next he sowed an offering. He offered 1000 burnt offerings to the Lord and remember in the first chapter we talked about money matters to God. Money moves God! When your honor is mixed with an offering God is moved and what happened next is amazing.

God appeared to Solomon that night and told him to ask for whatever he wanted. Wow that was miraculous. Solomon sowed 1000 offerings and God showed up that night. Don't tell me God isn't concerned about your giving.

Solomon asked for wisdom and God gave him that and then some. God gave him riches and honor as well as wisdom. The rest they say is history.

Solomon became the wisest and wealthiest King in all of history, all because he asked for the factory of favor, wisdom. People came from all over the world to absorb Solomon's wisdom. Someone who has something you don't have knows something you don't know. A man of God who has what you need knows some things that you don't. Absorb their wisdom and watch your life explode.

The next way to connect with a man of God is to follow his instructions. Every miracle has an instruction connected to it. Jesus did many miracles when He walked the earth 2000 years ago. Every miracle that He did came with an instruction.

He would tell someone to go show themselves to the priests, to another He would say "stretch out your hand." Still another He would tell to get up! Jesus gave instructions and if they were followed miracles started to happen.

A man of God may give you a crazy instruction but if you believe that He is the voice of God in your life than you will follow the instruction that He gives. On the other side of that is a miracle.

The prophet Elijah told the widow woman to make him a cake first and that her jar of flour and cruse of oil would never run out. This instruction seemed selfish and illogical but the miracle was on the other side of it.

An instruction may come in the form of a correction. Can you handle being corrected by a man of God? Everyone is doing something stupid. It is just a matter of whether or not we recognize it. Your man of God will see things that you do not see.

Correction is proof that you have a future. Jesus corrected Peter but not Judas. Peter had a future but Judas did not. Can you receive correction from a man of God without being offended? We are too close to ourselves to see what we need sometimes. A good protégé doesn't wait for his man of God to correct him but will as "what needs to be corrected in my life?" Correction is not a bad thing. It is necessary for advancement. Something you are doing or not doing is holding you back.

The story of Sheba in the Bible is one of my favorites. I Kings 10:1-5 tells us, *"When the queen of Sheba heard about the fame of Solomon and his relationship to the Lord, she came to test Solomon with hard questions. 2 Arriving at Jerusalem with a very great caravan with camels carrying spices, large quantities of gold, and precious stones, she came to Solomon and talked with him about all that she had on her mind. 3 Solomon answered all her questions, nothing was too hard for the king to explain to her. 4 When the queen of Sheba saw all the wisdom of Solomon and the palace that he had built, 5 the food on his table, the seating of his officials, the attending servants in their robes, his cupbearers, and the burnt offerings he made at the temple of the Lord, she was overwhelmed."*

What I love about this passage is that the queen of Sheba asked Solomon questions. The first key to following instructions and walking in wisdom is asking questions. Her questions unlocked King Solomon's instructions. We live in a society today where the famous are idiots and the wise are despised.

Not so in Solomon's day. His wisdom was pursued. You must pursue the mentorship and instructions of a man of God in order to prosper on the level that God wants you to prosper. The first thing that lets me know you want to learn is that you have a question.

The second thing that She did was give Solomon an offering. Verse 10 tells us that, *"She gave the King 120 talents of Gold, large quantities of spices, and precious stones. Never again were so many spices brought in as those the queen of Sheba gave to King Solomon."*

120 talents of Gold is 4 ½ tons of Gold. That amounts to more than $150,000,000 in today's economy. Now that is a gift! Which brings me to point number three. You must sow into a man of God's Anointing.

She couldn't leave without giving to Solomon. No wait a minute, shouldn't she have given that money to the poor. Solomon didn't need that money he already made 666 talents of gold per year which amount to 1.6 billion dollars per year.

That is right Solomon didn't need her money but she needed to give it. Solomon was not trying to get something from her but to give something to her. She was willing to connect to the blessing.

When you sow seeds of honor into your man of God it unlocks favor into your life. You are not doing him a favor you are doing yourself a favor. God didn't say believe a prophet because he needs some encouragement. He said believe a prophet so that you can prosper. A blessed man is mirror. Whatever you send his way is coming back to you multiplied. Sow where you want to go. In other words send your money in the direction of a blessed man. If you want to write books that touch the world send an offering to your favorite author. If you desire to have the best real estate firm in the south, send an offering to the number one realtor in your state.

You sow where you want to go. If you desire a blessed future and the fulfillment of God's purpose for your life, send a seed in the direction of a man of God ad watch miracles happen.

I have this one man in my ministry who is a consistent sower into my life. He has made more money in his paint contracting business than anyone I know. He has decided to partner with God by including me in his business.

A seed unlocks the financial blessing on a man of God's life. Every time I receive an offering from this man God gives me a word about contracts that are coming his way and sure enough within a few days his phone is blowing up.

It is something that I cannot explain. But it is supernatural. He sees me as a connection point to his business prospering. I have seen it in my own life. My own mentor and spiritual father has been that to me. I have sown thousands of dollars of seed into his life and

ministry and every time a harvest exploded in my life.
Plant your seed into good soil. Find a man of God that has an Anointing for prosperity on His life and sow your seed in his direction. That is a powerful key to unlocking a financial miracle. You must activate the third component in the equation of prosperity.
The next way to connect with a man of God is to serve his purpose. Get involved in the purpose of a man of God. What you make happen for others God will make happen for you. In other words find somewhere in his life that you can use your gift to help him.
Maybe it is driving him to where he needs to go or running security for his meetings. Serve the purpose of a man of God in some way. Use the gift that God has given you to elevate him and God will elevate you.
It reminds me of the story of Elijah and Elisha. Be an Elisha to a man of God in your life. Elisha poured water on the hands of Elijah for 14 years. He served him and ordered the natural so that Elijah could flow in the supernatural.
I want to shift here to a portion of my book The Ark, The Altar, and The Offering that explains the final three way to connect with a man of God more clearly. There is a scripture that I want us to look at in Jeremiah 3:15-16. It tells us, *15 And I will give you pastors according to mine heart, which shall feed you with knowledge and understanding.*

*16 And it shall come to pass, when ye be multiplied and increased in the land, in those days, saith the Lord, they shall say no more, The ark of the covenant of the Lord: neither shall it come to mind: neither shall they remember it; neither shall they visit it; neither shall that be done any more.*

Wow did you read that? This scripture tells us that the people will no longer follow The Ark or ask about it but God will give them Pastors according to His heart. Now you will no longer follow a gold covered box but you will follow my pastors or leaders that will give you knowledge and understanding.

So if there is no longer an Ark but now God has given us pastors we must deduce that whatever God put in The Ark He now will put in His leaders. The Ark had Aaron's rod that budded, the Jar of Manner, and the Ten Commandments. The Ten Commandments are the Message, Aaron's Rod or Staff that Budded was the Mantle, and The Jar of Manna was the Miracle.

So the Message, the Mantle, and the Miracle needed a new resting place and God decide to put them in His leaders, His pastors, His prophets. That's right your pastor is an Ark of God. Men of God are carriers of God's presence and they hold in them the Message, the Mantle, and the Miracle of God. Not because of who they are but because of who God is in them.

So no longer will a golden box lead God's people but men full of The Holy Ghost and power. So the next time you look at your pastor don't see a hired hand that preaches a good sermon. See Him as God sees him as an Ark of God's presence that possess a message, mantle, and miracle for you and your family.

We have replaced The Ark in our Churches with hirelings, motivational speakers, and life coaches. Nothing wrong with motivational speakers and life coaches it's just they don't belong on the Altar of God and they don't possess God's Message, His Mantle, or His Miracle.

God is raising up a generation of Kingdom Leaders and Pastors and Apostles that carry the Message, Mantle, and Miracle of God so that God's people can once again experience His Glory.

So let's take it a step further. Do we treat our pastor like an Ark or like a mere man? Remember Uzzah stretched his hand out and touched The Ark. How many of us touch our leader or try to tell him how it should be done? If the pastor is an Ark he should be honored like The Ark. Are you guiding him or are you letting Him guide you and train you? Seven attitudes that unlock the Message, Mantle, and Miracle in your pastor...

- Be Teachable
- Be Humble

- Be Generous
- Be Expectant
- Show Honor
- Be available to Serve
- Be Present

Some would argue with me that pastors are just men and we shouldn't put them on a pedestal. Well you put celebrities on pedestals and athletes on pedestals and they don't carry the Message, Mantle, or Miracle. God has elevated your Pastor, Bishop, or Apostle they are already on a pedestal and you didn't put them there, God did.

You just have to recognize it and change your perspective. God has chosen men to reveal Himself through and that was not our choice but his. Men are flawed and fallible but even David would not touch Saul when He has the opportunity to kill him.

Because He would not touch God's Anointed. Even though Saul had an evil spirit and was not serving God he was still Anointed King. And David honored him and God honored David for it. Your Pastor's flaws and weaknesses don't disqualify him from your respect and honor. He has a position in God and as The Ark was to be carried so you Pastor, Bishop, Apostle needs to be carried held up in prayer and support by showing honor.

The Bible says he who receives a prophet in the name of a prophet will receive a prophet's reward. If you perceive you will receive. What do I mean? Simple, I must first perceive you as a prophet before I can receive the prophet's reward. How do you perceive your pastor? As a hired hand that can be replaced if you don't like what he is doing and saying, or God's man for the hour in your Church who possesses a Mantle, Message, and Miracle that will bless your family.

# Chapter Review and Key Points

- The key to your financial future is a man of God. There is no logical explanation for it. God is logical but mysterious. You cannot figure Him out and once you do you have stopped following God and now created a false God in your mind.

- Someone who has something you don't have knows something you don't know. A man of God who has what you need knows some things that you don't. Absorb their wisdom and watch your life explode.

- When you sow seeds of honor into your man of God it unlocks favor into your life. You are not doing him a favor you are doing yourself a favor. God didn't say believe a prophet because he needs some encouragement. He said believe a prophet so that you can prosper. A blessed man is mirror. Whatever you send his way is coming back to you multiplied.

- Get involved in the purpose of a man of God. What you make happen for others God will make happen for you. In other words find somewhere in his life that you can use your gift to help him.

- Men of God are carriers of God's presence and they hold in them the Message, the Mantle, and the Miracle of God. Not because of who they are but because of who God is in them.

# ல 7 ය
# 100 Power Quotes About Covering

~~~~~

1. If a part of The BIBLE...
   ...is questioned
   ...criticized
   ...overlooked..
   ...explained away
   ...chances are you NEED that in your life...and you need to look into it DEEPER...
   #power
   #prosperity
   #pastorp

2. We LOST our authority...
   ...in a GARDEN (Eden)
   ...we got our authority BACK...
   ...in a GARDEN (Gethsemane)

#Jesus
#victory
#pastorp

3 When you tolerate REBELLION...you ALLOW people to TAKE you're AUTHORITY...and use it AGAINST you...
#takeyourplace

4 POWER is the ability to sit at the a TABLE with JUDAS...know that he is a JUDAS...and still talk to him like he's a DISCIPLE...[1]
#strategize

5 POWER is not being in a position to CONTROL...POWER is being in a position to HELP...
#pastorp

6 If you don't use your AUTHORITY...someone will take it and use it against you...#empowered

7 POWER without WISDOM...will destroy you...

---

[1] DMM 5001 Wisdom Quotations

8  POWER is the ABILITY to walk away from what you DESIRE...in order to PROTECT what you LOVE...

9  POWER is the man who CAN...but DOESN'T...

10 POWER...is when you CAN...but you DON'T...

11 The spirit of FANTASY...is robbing MEN of their AUTHORITY and disqualifying them from RESPONSIBILITY...
#truth

12 Jesus said "It is finished"...He didn't say "I Am finished"...meaning the work of redemption was COMPLETE on The CROSS...but He still had work to do in the TOMB...resurrecting and getting our keys of AUTHORITY back...

13 If your BAD choices don't AFFECT anyone...you're not that IMPORTANT...the more authority you have...the more people affected when you MESS UP...ask ADAM...

**14** You want to get A LOT of "LIKES"...post POPULAR words...you want to get FEW "LIKES"...post POWERFUL words...

**15** The BIBLE...
...the number ONE best-selling book in HISTORY...
...nuff SAID...
#GodsWord
#Inspired

**16** Either ALL of the BIBLE Is true...or NONE of it is...you can't pick and choose.

**17** The Word of God is a MIRROR...when you look into IT...you see a reflection of who you REALLY are!
#PastorP

**18** If The Bible has no power...then why is it the topic of discussion on MOST news networks? Why are there so many opposed to it. You don't ARGUE over something that has no IMPORTANCE...debate over GOD's WORD is PROOF of Its POWER...

**19** Some people love The Bible minus the BAD parts...hell, sin, judgment, sinner, stupid choices, goats...IT'S ALL OR NOTHING BABY!

**20** If you tell me you believe THE BIBLE is not TRUE...but you haven't read the WHOLE BOOK...you have no right to an opinion. Don't ever give an opinion about a book you haven't even READ...(read the whole Book and you'll be convinced it's God's WORD)

**21** For you that think The BIBLE condones drug use...STEPHEN getting STONED...is not a reference that will work for you...lol

**22** When you READ The Bible...The Bible will start READING YOU...[2]

**23** You cannot live for GOD...if you do not read His WORD...your spirit craves WORD...feed it...

**24** I've heard so many preachers lately teach that tithing is not New Testament...and we shouldn't do it. How MORONIC...Hebrews tells us Jesus is a Priest after the order of MELCHIZADOK...Abraham gave 10% of

---

[2] DMM 5001 Wisdom Quotations

his wealth to this priest. That was before the Mosaic Law. Based on Faith alone...that's Old and New Testament...read your BIBLES preachers...

**25** The very gallows that Haman built for MORDECAI...we're used on Haman himself...TRANSLATION: the weapon the enemy designed for you...will be the very weapon that takes him OUT...
#Word

**26** Our country is obsessed with defending the freedom of Muslims and other religions...but removing the freedom of Christians...The Bible has to be true because it's hated by so many...

**27** I wonder what would happen if we read the WORD...as much as we read FACEBOOK profiles...just a thought...

**28** The Word of God...ENDURES forever...#fallinlovewithHisWord

**29** We live in the most SPIRITUALLY gifted...yet BIBLICALLY illiterate generation ever...sad..

**30** God will not only bring you OUT...but His WORD will tell you how not to get INTO it...in the first place...save some TIME...

**31** Psalm 119:89 tells us that "God's Word is forever settled in HEAVEN"...but we must make sure IT is SETTLED on EARTH...and in US...

**32** God will bless what YOU do if you are committed and sold out...
...But if you're not you will sit back and watch him blessed what somebody ELSE does...
#spectators
#participators
#PastorP

**33** BLESSED doesn't mean the absence of PROBLEMS...but the wisdom and faith to find solutions...#youareblessed

**34** God didn't just call you to have a BLESSING...He called you to BE a BLESSING...blessing is not what I posses...it is who I am...I'd rather BE a BLESSING than have a Blessing any day...selah

**35** A BLESSED man is a mirror...whatever you send his way...will come back to you MULTIPLIED...

**36** Don't get SO blessed...that you forget who blessed you...GOTTA GIVE BACK!

**37** I'd rather be HATED for being BLESSED...than LOVED for being TOLERANT...

**38** You're being FOLLOWED...Psalm 23 declares "Surely goodness and mercy shall FOLLOW me ALL the days of my LIFE"...Start Chasing GOD and His BLESSING will start chasing you!

**39** God is not a celestial SANTA CLAUSE...He is The KING...He doesn't just want to give you a blessing...He's MAKING you a BLESSING...#beablessing

**40** You cannot curse...what God has BLESSED...#fact

**41** I can guarantee you that the fastest way to curse yourself...is to speak against a BLESSED man...

**42** The best thing you can do for the POOR...is not be one of them...[3]

**43** Why would God get mad at you for living in a NICE house and driving a nice CAR...when He lives in a TEMPLE and sits on a THRONE?...God's not intimidated by your BLESSING...

**44** "...forget not ALL His BENEFITS..."...serving GOD comes with a BENEFITS package...not Blue Cross Blue Shield...BUT...through the CROSS..."By His Stripes You were Healed..."

**45** INSPECTION...
...produces CORRECTION...
#pastorp

**46** Mentors provide CORRECTION...not AFFECTION...those who want your affection...often REJECT your correction...[4]

---

[3] DMM 5001 Wisdom Quotations
[4] DMM 5001 Wisdom Quotations

**47** The RIGHT people receive your correction...the WRONG people don't...

**48** Correction is a GIFT...you never correct someone that you see no potential in...correction means there's HOPE...in the relationship...

**49** We use our ENERGY to correct WRONG people...instead of celebrate RIGHT people...[5]

**50** Anything PERMITTED...INCREASES...love, hate, evil, deceit...[6]

**51.** Men of God...you're ASSIGNMENT is to raise up spiritual SONS...not CLONES...

**52.** ATTACK hits your LIFE...the MOMENT the enemy catches a WHIFF...of the FUTURE God has DESIGNED for YOU...

---
[5] DMM 5001 Wisdom Quotations
[6] DMM 5001 Wisdom Quotations

**53.** 2500 pastors LEAVE the ministry every day...not because they aren't COMPETENT...but because they're FATHERLESS...won't CONNECT to a spiritual FATHER...

**54.** My GREATEST struggle...TEACHING a NON-LEARNER...

**55.** Don't mistake my KINDNESS...for WEAKNESS...

**56.** I love PROACTIVE people...people who don't wait for YOU to tell them what to DO...but bring IDEAS to the table...whether they're used or not. Be PROACTIVE...not REACTIVE...

**57.** INCREASE requires more than just FAITH...it requires TRAINING...

58. You will KNOW the QUALITY of the RELATIONSHIP...when you see their REACTION... to The PRESENCE of God...

59. A FOOL can always remain HIDDEN...until he decides to OPEN his MOUTH...

60. POWER is the ability to sit at the a TABLE with JUDAS...know that he is a JUDAS...and still talk to him like he's a DISCIPLE...

61. FAMILIARITY...is a relationship KILLER...favor KILLER...honor KILLER...greatness KILLER...future KILLER...

62. You can DISOBEY me...and get AWAY with it...but you CANNOT disobey GOD...and get AWAY with it...

**63.** Your CHURCHES might be GROWING...but are the PEOPLE in your CHURCHES growing...?

**64.** The BIGGER your success...the BIGGER the problems you have to solve...

**65.** Stop telling God how big your PROBLEM is...start telling your problem...how BIG your GOD is...

**66.** You having a PROBLEM with ME...is not
     my PROBLEM...

**67.** How someone REACTS to my success...
...determines whether I want them to be part OF it...

**68.** Whatever you REACT to...
...you assigned IMPORTANCE to...

**69.** Your reaction to the UNCHANGING... determines what CHANGES in your life...

**70.** Study REACTIONS...
...it will AMAZE you...

**71.** A REACTION...
...is a DECISION...
...with no THOUGHT...

**72.** ANGER...
...is a FAVOR killer...

**73.** You reaction to a Man of GOD...
...DETERMINES God's reaction to you...

**74.** Most people don't THINK...
...past their FEELINGS...

**75.** We don't STUDY what's AROUND us...we REACT to what's around us...

76. God is STUDYING your REACTIONS...a reactor is volatile and unpredictable...but a RESPONDER takes powerful electric current...and CONVERTS it to a usable signal...are you a reactor...or a RESPONDER...?

77. Your REACTIONS reveal your MATURITY...when you REJECT the voices God puts in your life...you reveal your immaturity...

78. FEAR is the root...of every REACTION...FAITH is the root...of every RESPONSE...

79. Reactors are UNSTABLE...responders convert power to a USABLE signal...WHICH ARE YOU?

80. You REACTION to a Man of God...DETERMINES God's REACTION to you...

81. Don't ignore REACTIONS...there's too much INFORMATION in them...

82. We don't STUDY what's close to us...we REACT to what's close to us...

83. God trusted JOB because HE could predict JOB's reaction to attack before it happened...can GOD trust your REACTION in crisis...

84. There are two KINDS of people...those who REACT to what's close to them...and those who STUDY what's close to them...which one are you?

85. You don't KNOW someone...
...if you don't understand their DECISIONS...

86. Some things take a lot of TIME to BUILD...and no time to DESTROY...

87. Never work HARDER...
...than someone else is willing to WORK...meet them at their level of EFFORT...

88. Let the WRONG people go...
...they're keeping the RIGHT people hidden...

89. When WRONG people leave your life...
...RIGHT people enter...

90. If you are the one doing all of the GIVING...
...It's time for you to RE-EVALUATE the relationship...

91. If you don't let the WRONG people go...
...the RIGHT people won't show up...

92. A mans purpose is to HELP women...not help himself TO women...

93. Okay men you go ahead and stay home from church and send your wife and kids to church WITHOUT you....

...But don't get mad when your wife leaves you for another man who decided to be the PRIEST of his home...

94. RELATIONSHIPS move 3 things
Information
Money
Opportunity

95. Four kinds of people I IGNORE:

1) Those who criticize me
2) Those who don't trust me

3) Those to whom my words do not matter
4) Those who talk to me in an inappropriate tone...

**96.** Every relationship has a REWARD...
...when you LOSE sight of the reward...
...you lose the RELATIONSHIP...

**97.** If you CARE...
...you're THERE...
...period...

**98.** Somebody you LOVE...doesn't LIKE you.
Somebody you ENJOY...doesn't ENJOY you...

**99.** You have TWO kinds of PEOPLE in your LIFE...IRRIGATORS and IRRITATORS. Those who WATER your LIFE...and those who DON'T...

**100.** RELATIONSHIPS are like ELEMENTS on the periodic TABLE...you put the wrong ELEMENTS together...you get some DANGEROUS REACTION

# The Author

As a Bishop, Author, Coach, and Keynote speaker Paul Wondracek provides keynote speaking and future coaching in order to provide individuals, businesses, and leaders everywhere with momentum shifting strategies and training so that their lives, businesses and relationships can get *unstuck* and *forward focused*!

Paul's 20+ years of experience in leadership, mental and behavioral health counseling, and ministry have equipped him to speak powerfully into the lives of people who are experiencing life's struggles and stagnation in their forward progress.

Paul has the unique ability to *inspire* and *impart* wisdom and strategy into someone's present season that will shift their momentum and get their life moving in the right direction. He accomplishes this by assisting them in navigating through transitional seasons and getting them forward focused toward their dreams and goals.

With a Master's Degree and many great mentors and successes in his own life, Paul inspires others to take responsibility for their own success by being *transparent* about their own failures and shortcomings. Paul uses the experiences of his own struggles and challenges to help others get forward focused and shift their momentum out of stagnation and into their future.

Paul's endeavors to be a *Today Voice* helping others to create a *Tomorrow Mindset* Paul teaches leaders everywhere to create the future they want instead of tolerate the future they get.

Paul provides the highest level of service, mentorship, and coaching in order to help people achieve their dreams in order to develop a *No Retreat* mentality that will shift their momentum in the right direction.

**To Have Paul Wondracek speak at one of your next events...**

Contact us at info@momentumshifters.me

Or e-mail us at pastorptv@yahoo.com

*Make sure you check out other powerful books from Bishop Paul Wondracek!*

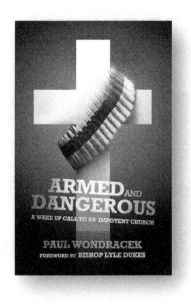

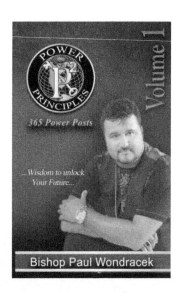

Made in the USA
Middletown, DE
24 August 2022